Coin

by Elena Ramone
illustrated by Robert McGuire

HOUGHTON MIFFLIN   BOSTON

Printed in China

ISBN 10: 0-618-88604-4
ISBN 13: 978-0-618-88604-3

15 16 17 18 19 0940 21 20 19 18 17
4500648149

Seth liked to do tricks. His best one was the
coin trick. Seth would ask for a quarter. Once he
had it, he would wave it around.

Read • Think • Write What is the value of a quarter?

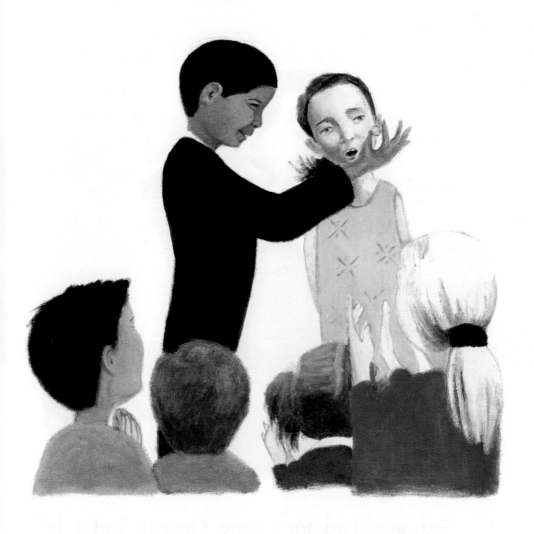

He would hide it up his sleeve. Then, he would pretend to find it behind someone's ear.

Read • Think • Write How many nickels equal a quarter?

Seth would ask for a dime. Once he had it, he would wave it around. Then he would hide it up his sleeve.

Read • Think • Write Is the value of a dime greater than, less than, or equal to a quarter?

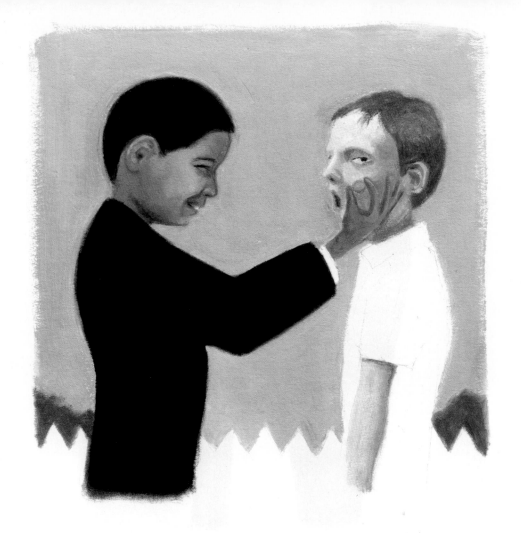

Then he would pretend to find it behind someone's ear.

"Ooh! Pull one from my ear!" a boy said.

Read • Think • Write How many nickels equal a dime?

"Do you have a nickel?" Seth asked.

Seth waved the boy's nickel around. Then he hid it up his sleeve.

Read • Think • Write What is the value of a nickel?

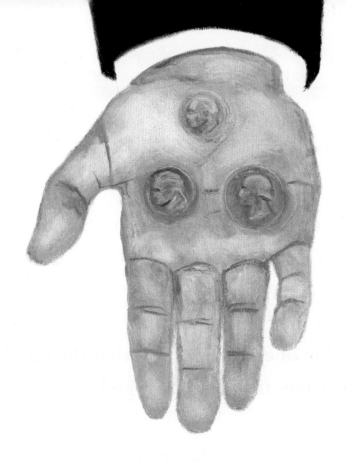

Seth pretended to find it behind the boy's ear.
"Ta-da!" said Seth.
"It's in your pocket," said the boy.
Seth turned red and pulled out the coins.

Read • Think • Write What is the value of all the
coins together?

Size Doesn't Matter

Show

Look at page 7. Draw the coins Seth is holding in his hand.

Share

Look at the coins on page 7. Talk about the value of each coin. Tell what the value of the coins are worth all together.

Write

Solve Problems/Make Decisions **Look at** page 7. Use ¢ to write the value of each coin.